EXPLORERS!

Ponce de León
Explorer of Florida

Arlene Bourgeois Molzahn

Enslow Publishers, Inc.

40 Industrial Road   PO Box 38
Box 398   Aldershot
Berkeley Heights, NJ 07922   Hants GU12 6BP
USA   UK

http://www.enslow.com

To my grandson, Daniel, my Eagle Scout.

Library of Congress Cataloging-in-Publication Data

Molzahn, Arlene Bourgeois.
    Ponce de León : explorer of Florida / Arlene Bourgeois Molzahn.
        p. cm. — (Explorers!)
    Summary: A biography of the Spanish explorer who first came to the New World with Columbus,
went on to become governor of Puerto Rico, and later came to Florida looking for the Fountain of Youth.
    Includes bibliographical references (p.) and index.
    ISBN 0-7660-2071-1
    1. Ponce de León, Juan, 1460?–1521—Juvenile literature. 2. Explorers—America—Biography—
Juvenile literature. 3. Explorers—Spain—Biography—Juvenile literature. 4. America—Discovery and
exploration—Spanish—Juvenile literature. [1. Ponce de León, Juan, 1460?–1521. 2. Explorers. 3. America—
Discovery and exploration—Spanish.] I. Title. II. Series: Explorers! (Enslow Publishers)
E125.P7M65 2003
972.9'02'092—dc21   2002014667

Printed in the United States of America

10 9 8 7 6 5 4 3 2 1

To Our Readers: We have done our best to make sure all Internet Addresses in this book were active and appropriate
when we went to press. However, the author and the publisher have no control over and assume no liability for the
material available on those Internet sites or on other Web sites they may link to. Any comments or suggestions can be
sent by e-mail to comments@enslow.com or to the address on the back cover.

Every effort has been made to locate all copyright holders of material used in this book. If any errors or omissions
have occurred, corrections will be made in future editions of this book.

Illustration credits: © 2002-2003 ArtToday.com, Inc., pp. 9, 10 (top), 19, 26, 38, 42; © 1999 Artville,
LLC., pp. 18, 36; Corel Corporation, pp. 10 (bottom), 13, 25, 33, 34, 38; Enslow Publishers, Inc., p.
24; Enslow Publishers, Inc. using © 1999 Artville, LLC. map, p. 27; Library of Congress, pp. 1, 4, 6, 7,
8, 9, 12, 14, 15, 16, 20, 21, 22, 28, 30, 32, 39, 40; Monster Zero Media, p. 41.

Cover Illustration: background, Monster Zero Media; portrait, Library of Congress.

Please note: Compasses on the cover and in the book are from © 1999 Artville, LLC.

Contents

Ponce de León set off to find the
Fountain of Youth. He never found
it, but he did discover Florida.

Into Battle

Juan Ponce de León was a Spanish explorer who discovered what is now Florida. He was searching for the Fountain of Youth. There were many tales about this fountain. Some people said the water from the fountain had the power to make old people young again. A young person who drank from the fountain would never grow old. Ponce de León never found the Fountain of Youth, but he did discover new lands.

No one knows much about the early years of Ponce de León. No one knows exactly when he was born. Many facts of this time were never written down or they have been lost.

Knights wore shining suits of armor.

Juan Ponce de León was born in the small town of Santervas de Campos in León, Spain. He was born probably between 1460 and 1474. His name was just Juan Ponce. Since he came from a royal family, his place of birth was added to his name. So he was called Juan Ponce de León.

As a boy, Ponce de León became a page to a Spanish knight, Don Pedro Nuñez de Guzmán. He lived with the

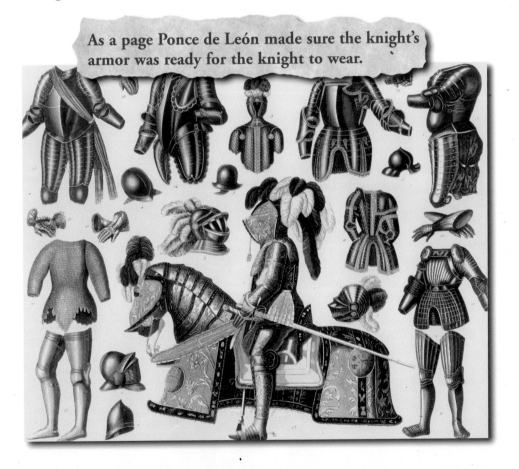

As a page Ponce de León made sure the knight's armor was ready for the knight to wear.

knight's family. He kept the knight's armor shining. He made sure the knight's other clothing was clean and ready for the knight to wear. He helped the knight dress and helped him get on his horse. He helped serve meals to the knight and his guests.

Ponce de León also had other chores to do. He helped set the table and took care of the candles in the house. He brought in wood for the many fireplaces. In return for working for the knight, Ponce de León was taught to read and write. He learned to hunt and how to ride a horse.

Armor was polished in shops like this one.

As a teenager, Ponce de León became a squire. He learned how to use different weapons so he would be ready to fight in battles, like this one.

Ponce de León was a page until he was about fifteen years old. Then, because he had done a good job, he became a squire. As a squire he had an important job to do. He had to take care of all the knight's weapons. Ponce de León learned to use swords and lances. He learned to fight while riding a horse. Then one day Ponce de León went into battle.

The Alhambra, a fortress and castle in Granada, Spain, was built by the Moors between 1248 and 1354. The Moors had been trying to take over Spain for many years. They were driven out in 1492 when Alhambra was captured by Spanish armies.

On Hispaniola

The Moors were people who were originally from northern Africa. They had been trying to take over Spain for more than one hundred years. Juan Ponce de León and Pedro Nuñez de Guzmán fought against the Moors. In 1492, the Moors were driven out of Spain and the war ended.

Ponce de León and the knight fought bravely. After the war ended, the knight was sent to teach the king's son. Ponce de León became a soldier in the Spanish army. He stayed in the army for about a year. Many people believe that Ponce de León joined explorer Christopher Columbus in 1493. Columbus was going

Christopher Columbus discovered new lands in 1492. Ponce de León may have set sail with Columbus in 1493 on Columbus's second voyage.

on his second voyage to the lands he had discovered in 1492.

By 1502, Ponce de León lived on the island of Hispaniola in the Caribbean Sea. Today the island is the home of two nations, Haiti and the Dominican Republic. Ponce de León married a Spanish woman named Leonor. They lived in Santo Domingo. This city was and is still an important seaport. Columbus arrived at that port during his fourth trip across the Atlantic Ocean.

Most explorers sailed in search of gold and spices. They hoped to get rich quickly and then sail back to their homes in Europe. Ponce de León decided to stay in Hispaniola and make money by farming. He had a large

Haiti

Haiti is a country in the West Indies. It is part of the island of Hispaniola. The other side of the island is the Dominican Republic. Port-au-Prince is Haiti's capital. Most people who live on Haiti are farmers. They raise beans, corn, rice, and yams. In the valleys and on the mountains of Haiti, people grow coffee, cacao (the bean used to make chocolate), and sugar cane.

Dominican Republic

The Dominican Republic is a country in the West Indies. It is part of the island of Hispaniola. The other side of the island is Haiti. Santo Domingo is the capital. There are many mountains in the Dominican Republic. Most people who live in rural areas are farmers. People who live in the cities earn a living by working in factories, for the government, or by fishing.

Both countries grow coffee. There are just two beans in each of these coffee berries.

People from the Taíno tribe were used as slaves to work on Ponce de León's farm. One of the crops grown was sugar cane.

farm, and he used people from the Taíno tribe as slaves to work on his farm. The Taíno are a part of a larger group of people called the Arawak. Ponce de León grew corn, sugar cane, sweet potatoes, and other crops. He raised pigs, cattle, and horses. He sold the goods to captains of the ships that came into Santo Domingo.

One important plant that Ponce de León grew was the cassava plant. The roots are used to make tapioca. They can also be eaten like potatoes. The roots are ground into flour to make bread.

People sailing back to Europe wanted cassava bread for the trip. Bread made with wheat flour spoiled quickly, but bread made with cassava flour lasted much longer. Cassava bread that was bought in Santo Domingo was still good when the ships reached Europe. Ponce de León did not have to hunt for gold to become a rich man. He became rich by staying on his farm and selling his farm goods.

The northeastern area of the island of Hispaniola was called Higüey. The Taíno who lived in Higüey were very unhappy. They did not want the Spaniards to take over the island. In 1504, there was an uprising. Ponce de León led his men in battle. There were more Taíno than Spaniards. But, the Spaniards had guns. The Taíno soon lost the battle.

Once the sugar cane was harvested, it was processed to make sugar.

Some of the Taíno were unhappy. They did not want the Spaniards to take over their lives and land. In 1504 there was an uprising. Even though there were more Taíno than Spaniards, the Taíno soon lost.

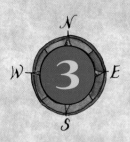

Governor
Ponce de León

After the battle, Ponce de León was named governor of that part of the island. Part of his job was to make sure the people who lived there had food, houses, and lessons in the Christian religion. King Ferdinand of Spain gave orders that the Taíno were to get paid for the work they did on the Spaniards' farms. But often they were paid very little or nothing at all.

Ponce de León heard about gold that was found on a nearby island, called Borinquén. Today this island is called Puerto Rico. He set sail on a secret trip to the island and found a small amount of gold. In 1508, King

Ponce de León heard about an island in the Caribbean Sea. Today that island is called Puerto Rico. He thought there may be gold on this island. This is what the map looks like today.

Ferdinand heard about the gold. He ordered Ponce de León to go to the island. He was to bring people to live there and begin searching for more gold.

As soon as he arrived on Puerto Rico, Ponce de León built a large stone house for himself, his wife, and their four children. The Arawak people who lived on the island helped. They built a town and a fort. They also planted crops on Ponce de León's farm. Then the Arawaks were put to work mining gold. Ponce de León soon became an even richer man. He was getting a share of the gold that was being mined. He also was making money selling goods grown on his farms in Hispaniola and in Puerto Rico. In 1509, King Ferdinand made Ponce de León the first governor of Puerto Rico.

Puerto Rico

Puerto Rico is an island southeast of Florida. San Juan is the capital of Puerto Rico. The name Puerto Rico means "rich port" in Spanish. Puerto Rico became a part of the United States in 1898. Puerto Ricans are citizens of the United States, but they cannot vote in presidential elections. They have their own local government on the island. Sugar cane and coffee are the main crops grown on the island.

San Juan, Puerto Rico, has many buildings that have Spanish influence.

Once Ponce de León landed in Puerto Rico he began to trade with the people who lived there. The Arawak people then helped to build a town and a fort.

After a while, the Spaniards took over the island of Puerto Rico and changed the way the Arawaks lived. This made the Arawaks angry. They did not like to farm, build houses, and mine gold for the Spaniards.

The Arawaks feared the Spaniards. They thought that the Spaniards were gods. But after a Spanish soldier was killed, the Arawaks were no longer afraid. If the Spaniards could die, then they were not gods. In 1511, the Arawaks attacked the Spanish settlers. Their stone axes were no match for the Spaniards' guns. The fight was soon over.

In Spain, in 1511, Diego Columbus met with the king of Spain. Diego Columbus was Christopher Columbus's oldest son. Christopher Columbus was promised he would be made governor of all the lands he discovered, but he died in 1506.

King Ferdinand kept his promise by making Diego Columbus governor of all the Spanish lands. Diego let his friends govern Hispaniola and Puerto Rico. This meant Ponce de León was no longer governor of Puerto Rico. But Ponce de León was allowed to keep his farms on the island.

King Ferdinand of Spain, seen here, made Diego Columbus governor of all Spanish lands that Christopher Columbus had discovered, including Puerto Rico.

Ponce de León landed on a beautiful beach. He called the land "La Florida."

"La Florida"

Ponce de León did not stay in Puerto Rico while Diego Columbus was governor. He had heard stories about a beautiful island north of Puerto Rico called Bimini. He also heard stories of a Fountain of Youth on the island whose waters made old people young again.

Ponce de León wanted to find Bimini. He asked King Ferdinand to let him explore the area. In 1512, the king agreed. He told Ponce de León that he would be made governor of all the lands that he discovered.

On March 3, 1513, Ponce de León and two hundred men left Puerto Rico. The explorers had three ships, the

Ponce de León's
First Voyage (1513)

Florida

Atlantic Ocean

Bahamas

Dry Tortugas

Cuba

Caribbean Sea

Cayman
Islands

Jamaica

Hispaniola

Santo
Domingo

Virgin
Islands

Puerto Rico

In 1513, Ponce de León sailed in search of the Fountain of Youth and found Florida. His route is shown here.

Santa Maria, the *Santiago*, and the *San Cristobal*. They sailed northwest.

On April 2, 1513, they landed on a beautiful sandy beach that they thought must be the island of Bimini. Birds, flowers, and butterflies made the land seem like a very pleasant place. Ponce de León called the land "La Florida." Florida means "flowery" in Spanish. Ponce de León arrived during the Easter season. So another story says that he named Florida after the Easter season which is "Pascua de Florida" in Spanish.

He planted a Spanish flag in the sandy beach and claimed the land he saw for Spain. We know now that this land was not an island. Ponce de León had reached the land that today is the state of Florida in the United States.

The explorers sailed farther along the coast and tried to land. But the people of the Ais tribe shot

Ponce de León and his men saw beautiful flowers, birds, and other animals when they landed in Florida. These are flamingoes.

Florida

In 1845, Florida became the twenty-seventh state in the United States. Its nickname is the Sunshine State because the weather is often sunny. Tallahassee is Florida's capital. Because of the warm weather, citrus fruits, such as oranges and grapefruits, grow well. Most of the frozen orange juice made in the United States is processed in Florida.

darts and arrows at the Spaniards and would not let them reach the shore.

On April 21, 1513, the three ships changed their course and began sailing south along the east coast of Florida. Suddenly, they sailed into a strong ocean current that slowed them down. The current was so powerful that it kept pushing the ships north even when the wind was blowing south. The ships put their anchors down and were still being carried toward the north.

Ponce de León had sailed into the Gulf Stream. The Gulf Stream is a warm, powerful ocean current. It begins in the Caribbean Sea and flows into the Gulf of Mexico. The current moves northeast along the coast of North

As Ponce de León was sailing around the coast of Florida, he sailed into the Gulf Stream. The Gulf Stream is a very powerful current. One of the captains, Antón de Alaminos took note of this current. He drew a map of the Gulf Stream years later. Ships sailing on the Gulf Stream from the Americas could reach Europe much faster.

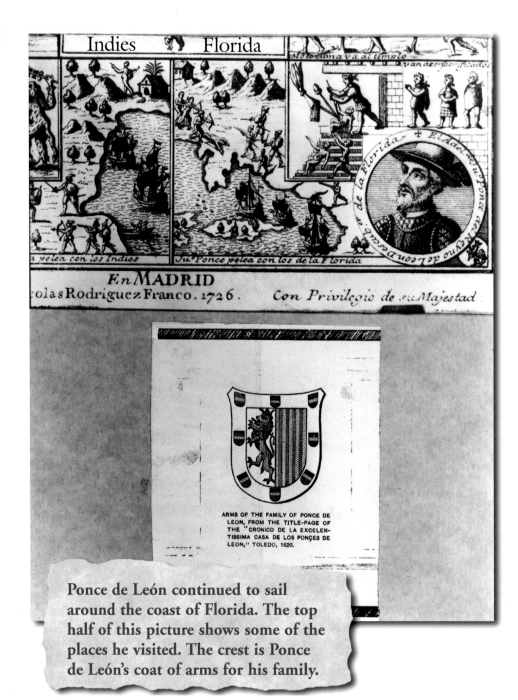

Indies   Florida

En MADRID
...olas Rodriguez Franco. 1726.   Con Privilegio de su Majestad

ARMS OF THE FAMILY OF PONCE DE
LEON, FROM THE TITLE-PAGE OF
THE "CRONICO DE LA EXCELEN-
TISSIMA CASA DE LOS PONÇES DE
LEON," TOLEDO, 1620.

Ponce de León continued to sail around the coast of Florida. The top half of this picture shows some of the places he visited. The crest is Ponce de León's coat of arms for his family.

America until it reaches Newfoundland, Canada. Then it becomes several currents that flow in different directions.

Antón de Alaminos knew this current was important. He was the captain of one of the other ships sailing with Ponce de León. Years later, Alaminos drew a map of the Gulf Stream. Ships sailing on the Gulf Stream from the Americas could reach Europe much faster. The Gulf Stream became an important trade route.

Finally, Ponce de León and a few of his men were able to row ashore in the ship's small boat. The Ais watched from the shore. A group of them tried to take the small boat after it landed. Ponce de León did not want to fight. He hoped the Ais could help him in his search for gold and the Fountain of Youth. But they shot their bows and arrows. One of the explorers was hurt. The Spaniards hurried back to the small boat and rowed to the ship.

The ships kept sailing south and west around the southern tip of Florida.

Prom.Lupi.

Portus Regalis,siue F.S.Helenæ.

5

Turtles and an Old Woman

The explorers continued to sail south along the east coast of Florida. As the ships sailed along the coast, the Ais were always ready to attack. So the Spaniards could not go ashore to do any exploring.

The ships kept sailing south and west around the southern tip of Florida. On May 8, 1513, they stopped at a small group of islands southwest of Florida. No one lived there but many, many sea turtles were found on these islands. Ponce de León named the islands Tortugas Islands, which in Spanish means "tortoise islands." He added the word "dry" to the name because they could not find fresh water on the islands. Today the islands are still known as the Dry Tortugas Islands.

On July 18, 1513, the explorers anchored their ships at another small island along the southwest coast of Florida. The men went ashore to get fresh water. They were surprised to find an old woman living alone on the island. They thought it would be better for the woman if they brought her to Puerto Rico to live. They also

They found a small island along the southwest coast of Florida. Ponce de León and his men stopped to find fresh water.

thought the woman might know about the area in which they were sailing. Ponce de León was sure the Fountain of Youth was not on this island because the woman was very old.

Ponce de León and his men found many islands on their voyage of discovery. But they did not know anything about the lands. The many people who lived on the lands would not let the Spaniards explore. So the explorers knew very little about the lands they had seen.

They reached Cuba and the Yucatán Peninsula of Mexico

Ponce de León and his men were able to find fresh water on the islands they explored.

Long before Europeans explored the Yucatán Peninsula of Mexico, Maya Indians lived there. This picture shows some ancient Maya ruins.

before they sailed back to Puerto Rico. On October 19, 1513, Ponce de León and his ships returned home.

The explorers had been gone for almost eight months. Many things had happened in Puerto Rico while they were away. The new governor had made the Arawak people very angry. He had allowed the Spaniards to take over land that did not belong to them.

On June 2, 1513, the Arawak had attacked Caparra, Puerto Rico. This is the town where Ponce de León and his family lived. The town was burned to the ground. When Ponce de León arrived home he found his house was gone. Luckily, his wife and their four children were safe.

Ponce de León went to Spain to tell King Ferdinand about all the lands he had discovered. The king was pleased with Ponce de León and made him a knight.

6

The Last Battle

In April 1514, Ponce de León went to Spain to meet with King Ferdinand. He gave the king a report of the new lands that had been discovered. Ponce de León also wanted to please the king. Since he had not found gold during his explorations, he brought some of his own gold to King Ferdinand.

All of the islands that Ponce de León had discovered were placed on official maps and claimed for Spain. The king also gave Ponce de León the right to start a settlement in Florida. On September 27, 1514, the king named Ponce de León the governor of that land. He said that Ponce de León would get a share of all the gold that was discovered. He would also get a share of all the money that was earned by trading goods from the new lands.

Finally, King Ferdinand made Ponce de León a knight. Ponce de León's name became Don Juan Ponce de León.

On May 14, 1515, Ponce de León left Spain and sailed back to Puerto Rico. He reached Puerto Rico on July 15, 1515. He wanted to start a settlement in Florida. Instead, he was

Ponce de León sailed back to Puerto Rico to get supplies to start a settlement in Florida.

asked to lead an army to fight the Carib tribe who lived on the islands near Puerto Rico. They were fierce fighters and would often attack the settlers in Hispaniola and in Puerto Rico. Ponce de León and his soldiers fought the Caribs from 1515 until 1521. In 1519, while Ponce de León was fighting the Caribs, his wife died.

Finally, on February 21, 1521, Ponce de León sailed

In February 1521, Ponce de León finally made it to the west of Florida to start a settlement.

to Florida to start a settlement. He had two ships that were loaded with horses, cattle, sheep, pigs, and chickens. The ships also carried food, plants, seeds, and tools for farming. Over two hundred people were on the ships; among them were farmers, soldiers, and priests.

The Spaniards began building a settlement on the west coast of Florida. On July 1, 1521, a group of angry people from the Calusa

In July 1521, a group of angry Calusa men attacked. Ponce de León was struck in the leg with an arrow and was badly hurt. He died a few days later.

Ponce de León is known as the "Father of Puerto Rico." Shown here is the fort El Morro in San Juan. The El Morro Fortress was built by Spaniards about eighteen years after Ponce de León's death.

tribe attacked the workers. Ponce de León was struck in the leg with an arrow. He was badly hurt. His men carried him to a ship and sailed to the nearest Spanish settlement in Cuba. The second ship, loaded with the remaining settlers, left Florida to return to Puerto Rico.

Doctors did not have the kinds of medicine that we have today. They could not stop the infection from the arrow wound in Ponce de León's leg. He died a few days later.

Ponce de León is known as the "Father of Puerto

Rico." He discovered gold and started a settlement. He became the island's first governor.

He never did find the Fountain of Youth. But Ponce de León was the first European to discover Florida and the many islands along its coast. He claimed the newly discovered lands for Spain.

Today, the Dry Tortugas Islands are a United States National Park. The unusual birds and sea life that the Spaniards saw on these islands can still be seen and enjoyed today.

Fort Jefferson, located in Dry Tortugas National Park, was built between 1846 and 1866 to protect the United States. The park is also home to many types of sea life.

Timeline

1460–1474—Juan Ponce de León is born some time between these years.

1508—Spanish settlers begin a settlement in Puerto Rico.

1509—Is appointed the first governor of Puerto Rico.

1513—Is the first European to reach Florida; the first European to discover and name the Dry Tortugas Islands.

1514—Is made governor of Florida.

1521—Ponce de León dies in Havana, Cuba.

1909—The body of Ponce de León is returned to Puerto Rico and reburied in the cathedral in San Juan, Puerto Rico.

Words to Know

cassava—A plant grown in warm lands in the Americas. The roots are used to make tapioca, are eaten like potatoes, or are ground into flour.

continent—A very large body of land. The continents of the world are: Asia, Africa, Europe, North America, South America, Antarctica, and Australia.

expedition—A journey or voyage taken for a special reason.

governor—A person who governs, or rules, an area.

infection—Something that causes illness or something that causes illnesses to spread.

lance—A long wooden spear with a very sharp end.

peninsula—A long arm of land with water around it on three sides.

seaport—Also called a port; A place where ships can load and unload.

Learn More About
Ponce de León

Books

Hurwicz, Claude. *Juan Ponce de León*. New York: Rosen Publishing Group, 2001.

Kline, Trish. *Ponce de León*. Vero Beach, Fla.: Rourke Publishing, 2002.

Knotts, Bob. *Florida History*. Chicago, Ill.: Heinemann Library, 2002.

Kummer, Patricia K. *Puerto Rico*. Minnetonka, Minn.: Capstone Press, Inc., 2002.

Sakurai, Gail. *Juan Ponce de Leon*. Danbury, Conn.: Scholastic Library Publishing, 2002.

Learn More About
Ponce de León

Internet Addresses

Juan Ponce de León: Explorer

<www.enchantedlearning.com/explorers/page/d/deleon.shtml>

Learn more about Ponce de León.

Dry Tortugas National Park

<www.nps.gov/drto/index.htm>

Read about the history of the Dry Tortugas.

Index

Moors, 10, 11

N
Newfoundland, Canada, 29
North America, 27, 29
Nuñez de Guzmán, Pedro,
    7, 11

P
Ponce de León, Leonor, 12
Puerto Rico, 17, 18, 19, 20,
    21, 23, 32, 35, 38, 39, 41

S
San Cristobal, 24
San Juan, 19
Santa Maria, 24

Santervas de Campos, Spain, 7
Santiago, 24
Santo Domingo, 12, 13, 14, 15
Spain, 7, 10, 11, 17, 21, 25,
    36, 37, 38, 42

T
Taíno tribe, 12, 14, 15, 16, 17

U
United States, 19, 25, 26
United States National Park, 42

W
West Indies, 13

Y
Yucatán Peninsula, 33